Johann Joachim QUANTZ

(1697 – 1773)

Concerto for Flute, Strings and Basso continuo
QV 5 : 174
G Major / Sol majeur / G-Dur

Piano Reduction by
Gero Stöver

DOWANI International

Preface

This edition presents a piece that belongs in the standard repertoire of every flutist: the Concerto for flute, strings and basso continuo QV 5:174 in G Major by Johann Joachim Quantz. It allows you to work through the piece systematically and at different tempi with accompaniment.

The CD begins with the concert version of each movement. After tuning your instrument (Track 1), the musical work can begin. First, you will hear the piano accompaniment at slow and medium tempo for practice purposes. At slow tempo you can also hear the flute played softly in the background as a guide. Having mastered these levels, you can now play with orchestral accompaniment at the original tempo. Only in the concert version is the cadenza played complete. The practice tempos give you time to play a very short cadenza; the entrance following the cadenza can be found with the aid of a metronome click. All of the versions were recorded live. The names of the musicians are listed on the last page of this volume; further information can be found in the Internet at www.dowani.com.

We wish you lots of fun playing from our *DOWANI 3 Tempi Play Along* editions and hope that your musicality and diligence will enable you to play the concert version as soon as possible.

It is our goal to give you the essential conditions for effective practicing through motivation, enjoyment and fun.

Your DOWANI Team

Avant-propos

Cette édition vous présente un morceau qui fait partie du répertoire standard de tous les flûtistes : le concerto pour flûte, cordes et basse continue QV 5 : 174 en Sol majeur de Johann Joachim Quantz. Cette édition vous offre la possibilité de travailler l'œuvre d'une manière systématique dans différents tempos avec un accompagnement professionnel.

Le CD vous permettra d'entendre d'abord la version de concert de chaque mouvement. Après avoir accordé votre instrument (plage N° 1), vous pourrez commencer le travail musical. Pour travailler le morceau au tempo lent et au tempo moyen, vous entendrez l'accompagnement de piano. Au tempo lent, la flûte restera cependant toujours audible très doucement à l'arrière-plan. Vous pourrez ensuite jouer le tempo original avec accompagnement d'orchestre. La cadence entière a été enregistrée seulement dans la version de concert. Aux tempos de travail, vous aurez le temps de jouer une très brève cadence ; le métronome vous aidera à trouver l'attaque après la cadence. Toutes les versions ont été enregistrées en direct. Vous trouverez les noms des artistes qui ont participé aux enregistrements sur la dernière page de cette édition ; pour obtenir plus de renseignements, veuillez consulter notre site Internet : www.dowani.com.

Nous vous souhaitons beaucoup de plaisir à faire de la musique avec la collection *DOWANI 3 Tempi Play Along* et nous espérons que votre musicalité et votre application vous amèneront aussi rapidement que possible à la version de concert.

Notre but est de vous offrir les bases nécessaires pour un travail efficace par la motivation et le plaisir.

Les Éditions DOWANI

Vorwort

Mit dieser Ausgabe präsentieren wir Ihnen ein Stück, das zum Standardrepertoire eines jeden Flötisten zählt: das Konzert für Flöte, Streicher und Basso continuo QV 5:174 in G-Dur von Johann Joachim Quantz. Diese Ausgabe ermöglicht es Ihnen, das Werk systematisch und in verschiedenen Tempi mit Begleitung zu erarbeiten.

Auf der CD hören Sie zuerst die Konzertversion eines jeden Satzes. Nach dem Stimmen Ihres Instrumentes (Track 1) kann die musikalische Arbeit beginnen. Zum Üben folgt nun im langsamen und mittleren Tempo die Klavierbegleitung, wobei im langsamen Tempo die Querflöte als Orientierung leise im Hintergrund zu hören ist. Anschließend können Sie sich im Originaltempo vom Orchester begleiten lassen. Die Kadenz wird nur in der Konzertversion komplett gespielt. Bei den Übe-Tempi haben Sie jeweils Zeit für eine sehr kurze Kadenz; den Einsatz nach der Kadenz finden Sie mit Hilfe von Metronomklicks. Alle eingespielten Versionen wurden live aufgenommen. Die Namen der Künstler finden Sie auf der letzten Seite dieser Ausgabe. Ausführlichere Informationen können Sie im Internet unter www.dowani.com nachlesen.

Wir wünschen Ihnen viel Spaß beim Musizieren aus *DOWANI 3 Tempi Play Along*-Ausgaben und hoffen, dass Ihre Musikalität und Ihr Fleiß Sie möglichst bald bis zur Konzertversion führen werden.

Unser Ziel ist es, Ihnen durch Motivation, Freude und Spaß die notwendigen Voraussetzungen für effektives Üben zu schaffen.

Ihr DOWANI Team

Concerto

for Flute, Strings and Basso continuo, QV 5:174
G Major / Sol majeur / G-Dur

J. J. Quantz (1697 – 1773)
Piano Reduction: G. Stöver

6

Johann Joachim QUANTZ

(1697 – 1773)

Concerto for Flute, Strings and Basso continuo
QV 5 : 174
G Major / Sol majeur / G-Dur

Flute / Flûte traversière / Querflöte

DOWANI International

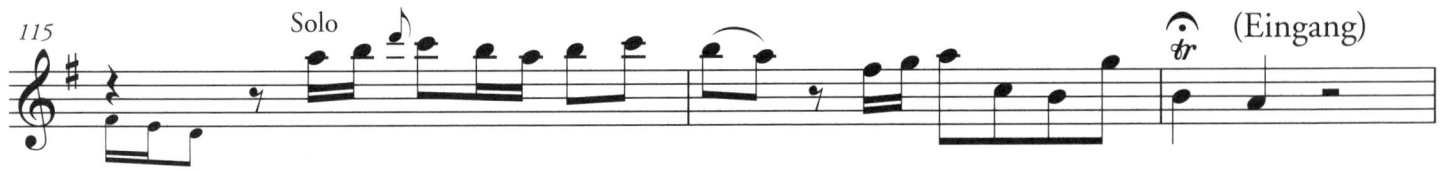

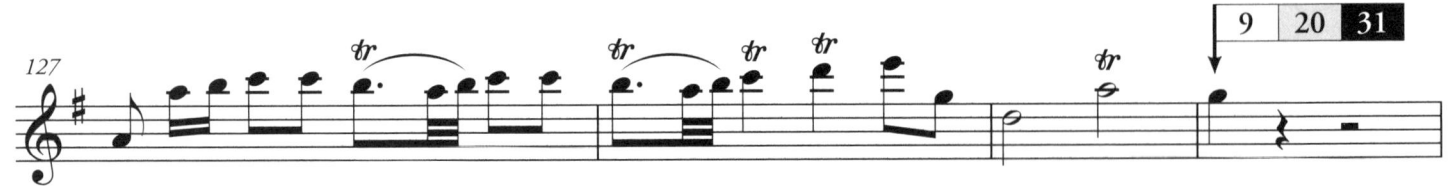

25

ENGLISH

DOWANI CD:
- Track No. 1
- Track numbers in circles
- Track numbers in squares

1 - tuning notes
● - concert version

- slow Play Along Tempo
- intermediate Play Along Tempo
- original Play Along Tempo

- Additional tracks for longer movements or pieces
- **Concert version:** flute and orchestra
- **Slow tempo:** piano accompaniment with flute in the background
- **Intermediate tempo:** piano accompaniment only
- **Original tempo:** orchestra only

Please note that the recorded version of the piano accompaniment may differ slightly from the sheet music. This is due to the spontaneous character of live music making and the artistic freedom of the musicians. The original sheet music for the solo part is, of course, not affected.

Cadenzas: The full cadenzas are only played in the concert version.

FRANÇAIS

DOWANI CD:
- Plage N° 1
- N° de plage dans un cercle
- N° de plage dans un rectangle

1 - diapason
● - version de concert

- tempo lent play along
- tempo moyen play along
- tempo original play along

- Plages supplémentaires pour mouvements ou morceaux longs
- **Version de concert :** flûte avec accompagnement d'orchestre
- **Tempo lent :** accompagnement de piano avec flûte en fond sonore
- **Tempo moyen :** seulement l'accompagnement de piano
- **Tempo original :** seulement l'accompagnement de l'orchestre

L'enregistrement de l'accompagnement de piano peut présenter quelques différences mineures par rapport au texte de la partition. Ceci est dû à la liberté artistique des musiciens et résulte d'un jeu spontané et vivant, mais n'affecte, bien entendu, d'aucune manière la partie soliste.

Cadences: Les cadences entières ont été enregistrées seulement dans la version de concert.

DEUTSCH

DOWANI CD:
- Track Nr. 1
- Trackangabe im Kreis
- Trackangabe im Rechteck

1 - Stimmtöne
● - Konzertversion

- langsames Play Along Tempo
- mittleres Play Along Tempo
- originales Play Along Tempo

- Zusätzliche Tracks bei längeren Sätzen oder Stücken
- **Konzertversion:** Flöte und Orchester
- **Langsames Tempo:** Klavierbegleitung mit Flöte im Hintergrund
- **Mittleres Tempo:** nur Klavierbegleitung
- **Originaltempo:** nur Orchester

Die Klavierbegleitung auf der CD-Aufnahme kann gegenüber dem Notentex kleine Abweichungen aufweisen. Dies geht in der Regel auf die künstlerische Freiheit der Musiker und auf spontanes, lebendiges Musizieren zurück. Die Solostimme bleibt davon selbstverständlich unangetastet.

Kadenzen: Die Kadenzen sind nur in der Konzertversion komplett eingespie

---

DOWANI - 3 Tempi Play Along is published by:
DOWANI International Est.
Industriestrasse 24 / Postfach 156, FL-9487 Bendern,
Principality of Liechtenstein
Phone: ++423 370 11 15, Fax ++423 370 19 44
Email: info@dowani.com
www.dowani.com

Recording & Digital Mastering: Pavel Lavrenenkov, Russia
CD-Production: Sonopress, Germany
Music Notation: Notensatz Thomas Metzinger, Germany
Design: Atelier Schuster, Austria
Printed by: Buchdruckerei Lustenau, Austria
Made in the Principality of Liechtenstein

Concert Version
Giulio Giannelli Viscardi, Flute
Russian Philharmonic Orchestra Moscow
Boris Perrenoud, Conductor

3 Tempi Accompaniment
Slow
Tatyana Gevorkova, Piano

Intermediate
Tatyana Gevorkova, Piano

Original
Russian Philharmonic Orchestra Moscow
Boris Perrenoud, Conductor

© DOWANI International. All rights reserved. No part of this publication may be reproduced, stored, in a retrieval system, or transmitted in any form or by any means, electronic, mechanical, photocopying, recording, or otherwise, without the prior permission of the publisher.